METAVERSE MANIFESTO
Orange Montagne

D1126451

Manufactured in the United States of America.

Montagne, Orange, 2007

Metaverse Manifesto.

ISBN 978-0-6151-4443-6

We shall fabricate these new lands
- with new meaning.

We declare this a new land
- with new inhabitants.

We declare this a new way of being
- with new purpose.

Note on this edition:

This is a "root text". Obviously, it is patterned after (or derived from) another famous Manifesto - this is done for dramatic and entertainment effect.

Cover illustration:

Features building by Analogue Montagne, fashion design by Acedia Albion, and Indigo Paperclip as photographed by Orange Montagne.

Thanks:

This book was written entirely while logged into virtual worlds. So, I want to thank the makers of virtual worlds for generating the vision and space for this creativity and social phenomenon to flourish. Thanks also to all the Avatars I have met so far inside virtual worlds.

Orange Montagne

This book is for Avatars.

THE DIGITAL LANDSCAPE IS REALIZED

A spectre is haunting the mind of the industrialized world - the spectre of the virtual.

All the powers of commerce have entered into a holy alliance to control this spectre: namely, corporations and "governments".

Where is there a reality that has not been decried as "virtual" and invalid by the forces that wish to control these realities?

There are two factors emerging.

I. The Metaverse is already acknowledged by corporate entities to be itself a phenomenon.

II. It is high time that the creators of realities should openly, in the face of the whole world, publish their views, their aims, and meet this legendary time with a Manifesto of the Metaverse itself.

To this end, the Metaverse Manifesto emerges.

METAVERSE MANIFESTO

I. REALITY AND ILLUSION ON
THE DIGITAL LANDSCAPE

II. REALITY IS THE ONLY COMMODITY

III. A COUP OF PERCEPTION

IV. REDUCTIONIST REACTIONS

V. YOU HAVE BEEN AUGMENTED

1. REALITY AND ILLUSION ON THE DIGITAL LANDSCAPE

There is no objective reality whatsoever. There never has been.

Realities have always stood in opposition to one another - in uninterrupted struggle - requiring the complete revolutionary construction of one reality and the ruin of its opposition.

In earlier epochs of history, we find everywhere a complicated arrangement of societies structured around perceived and subsequently enforced realities.

Humans have already split into two camps - those that cling to the dim vestiges of a default "reality" and those that are forging new, augmented realities.

From the time that art and writing emerged, these two camps have been in opposition - constructed, destroyed, and reconstructed.

The default realities generally grasped onto by the governors of persons and the new realities desired by the governed.

The improvement of computing technologies has opened up the airwaves, the transmission lines, and now the very channels of commerce themselves to a new class, namely, Reality-creators.

The feudal system of industry, under which industrial production was monopolized by closed corporations, now no longer suffices for the growing wants of the new markets.

Yet the reality masters of the past are not yet pushed aside - they continue to divide the creators and consumers as governors and the governed - as producer and consumer.

Meanwhile, as the data transmission lines have opened up - ideas have been disseminated - new venues have been created.

As these venues are created, the old guard corporate entities struggle to "acquire" them - with prices reflecting their intense desire to control.

The personal computer has enabled a decentralized world-market - for which the development and freedom of the internet has paved the way.

This market has given immeasurable benefits and riches to the general population - everyone has benefited.

Although the technologists have created the infrastructure for this market - the Reality-creators have given its vitality and meaning.

Although the developers of this set of technologies pre-existed within corporations, the fictional persons became increasingly incapable of creating any meaningful content for the venues they owned.

We have lived for decades under an iron fist of top-down mass media edicts from faceless inhuman "corporations" and "governments".

We have lived under the realities that these powers saw fit to prescribe for the consumers of them.

This system has converted the genius into the slave, the poet into the lackey, the man of science into the minion.

This system has torn away from the family its essential connections, and reduced the exchange of profound ideas to "entertainment."

This system of reality domination has existed for eons - as long as the value of realities has been known by those in power.

The "corporate" system entered its own dominant stage, with these fictional bodies engaged in vicious struggles, always towards a complete monopoly and a complete control.

Too often the consumer, the individual, and in time - reality itself - became casualties in these wars.

These corporations cannot exist without constantly recreating their own meaningful existence in the consumer's life. In doing so they seek a relationship with the individual and her realities.

The pursuit of controlling this reality leads to ever-intensified means of "branding" – literally charring the chosen images into the wandering mind of the "target".

Whenever a reality arises that competes with a corporate reality - it must be assimilated or better yet, destroyed. There is no option of co-existence with the corporate entity's realities.

The intellectual creations of real people had become corporate property - corporations that then plot against those very creators themselves.

This resolute and sustained action compels all nations, on pain of extinction, to adopt the reality on offer by the general conglomerate.

It has created a static menu of content - a cyclic churning of images - a regurgitated amalgam of tried and true concepts.

This system has forced entire generations to become "lowest common denominators". This system has forced intellect out entirely from public view - as if obscene.

Although the system has created realities that are inhabited and temporarily valid in their own right, this is largely due to their monopolistic hold. The receiver remained without option in the marketplace that was billed as "open."

We see then, that the means of experiencing reality itself were gradually "acquired", and then monopolized by mainstream media and corporations.

Into their place has stepped "the virtual".

This movement is growing before our eyes - on our "small screens".

Big money controls the big screen. Big money controls the blue screen. Individuals control the flat screen.

The corporate realities are like spells of a weakened sorcerer, now no longer able to control the nether world dwellings of the fabric of reality itself.

The seams are showing. Its monolithic whole is breaking into pieces. The source and power of realities is shifting, becoming ubiquitous, ambient, infinitely variable.

All creativity in human history has been a revolt against a prevailing reality.

The conflict of perceived realities creates a market struggle - and this creates a physical struggle – over the resources to feed these given realties.

Here it is obvious that reality itself is the commodity sought - the very object of desire.

At this time now, the small screen media - dominated by individuals - stands in stark contrast to the decaying and flickering monopolistic reality morsels sifted out to the viewers by the corporations.

One is alive - the other is dead.

One has meaning - the other has lost meaning.

One is "real" - the other is a broadcast illusion.

Wherever possible, the "consumer" never hesitates to turn the means of information dissemination back on the controller.

We have seen this revolt time and time again as technology became affordable to the masses.

The consumer is only too happy to do it.

And, amongst these ordinary folk, emerge those willing and able to wage this struggle, and here they are called Reality-creators.

Where before she was counted as just an "eyeball" now she must be counted as an equal.

Where before she was passive, she has now become active.

Where before she consumed - now she produces.

Where before she was deprived the means of reality production - now it is her very reality that she herself shapes and makes meaningful.

The system whereby this powerlessness had been garnered needs no further criticism - it has already been shunned. It has already been dismissed.

At its most basic sense - "realty" had been superseded by "illusion".

At its most basic sense - corporations were the only "people" that mattered.

No more.

Did you know anyone who craved a "branding experience"?

Did you know anyone who had been passionately inspired by a corporate entity?

We have entered the time in which the controls are slowly - slowly - bit by bit - being returned to the individual. The individual now has more power than ever before in human history.

We enter now the time in which the reality or illusion - whichever you choose to name the experience - can all be chosen, changed, selected, deselected, manipulated, and ultimately - disposed of.

The circle is now complete.

From corporate worlds to "End user" worlds.
"End user" created qualities.
"End user" created experiences.

"End user" created meaning.

"End user" created reality.

These realities will be created by "so-called" amateurs. We already have the first "crowdsourced" media channels and multiplayer worlds.

Like ants in the colony each moves a small piece to create the colony.

Until now only few individuals had this power. They were the elite few "trained" artists installed at or promoted by corporations.

Even those were constrained and bound by the work of warfare for monopoly and the curses of democratic vote.

A tasteless morass ensued. The morass falls out of view, rejected.

All previous art was created as a reaction against prevailing realities.

A movement of one or a small group - and an individual or small group that moves, always found itself sharply pitted against the corporate entities.

Conflict is inevitable in a skirmish to determine the parameters of reality.

The artist and the individual must rise up to be visible - and the violent overthrow of the corporate realities must follow.

It is just these upheavals which have defined history itself.

We can no longer live under corporate realities - in other words, their existence is no longer relevant - is no longer meaningful.

The essential condition for the existence and rise of the Reality-creators is the formation and then further augmentation of virtual worlds.

What the corporations produce, above all, became their own recycled cultures. Their realities' fall and the victory of the Reality-creators are equally inevitable.

The illusion from this point forward will be a chosen illusion.

There is no objective reality whatsoever.

There never has been.

Entering this mixed-reality - entering this flowing stream of exchanged images - delivers the observer from the tyranny of the top-down default prescribed reality.

This media liberates by its own method of action - the perceiver becomes the most crucial part of the perception.

What emerge from this series of struggles are completely formed new places - now called "virtual worlds".

The advance of this state requires violence - a violence of perception - into which we have already vaulted happily.

The advance of this state requires a chaos - a chaos barely containable - through which we are already navigating.

We shall fabricate these new lands
- with new meaning.

II. REALITY IS THE ONLY COMMODITY

In what relation do humans stand within the Metaverse as a whole?

Humans do not form a separate group apart from Avatars.

In fact, humans are Avatars.

Humans do not have any interests apart from - or rights divisible from - the Avatar.

The world the Avatar now inhabits, is the world the human will soon inhabit.

Each manifestation of the being - human - Avatar - spaceship or other virtual representation will have the same interests unless voluntarily constrained within a known game reality.

The immediate aim of the Reality-creators is the formation worlds for these beings, which form a uniquely perceptive and powerful class.

This class has one aim - that by creating realties and worlds that the power of reality creation remains distributed to the individual.

This movement has no aim that is historically different from those of artists or visionaries of prior times.

The creation of one's own realities is not at all a distinctive feature of a Metaverse.

Sharing that reality with others through this new interconnected medium however - in a matter of instants without physical contact – this is the palpable revolution which is at hand.

In this new medium, property is tangible as experience.

In this new medium, property is tangible as images and the ability to replay those images.

In this new medium, wealth is finding new measure in one or more of these abilities.

Many more measures of wealth and property are opening up as a result of this revolution.

The distinguishing feature of the Reality-creators is the ability to wage battle against the corporate entities for control of the reality fields - or the Metaverse.

In this sense the theory of the Metaverse Manifesto can be summed up in a single sentence:

Reality is the only commodity.

Creation and augmentation of this reality represents the basis of all personal freedom, activity and independence.

Hard-won, self-acquired, self-earned reality!
Do you mean the reality of the humble individual creator?
That is what is emerging now.

Or, do you mean the reality of the corporate entity?
That is what is fading - now even as we speak.

It has been no secret that the corporate aims in using these channels were to dominate the viewer.

It has been no secret that they have worked hand in hand with "news" disseminators to steer their messages and realities.

We know that this old media was created for this purpose - hence, it has no purpose in the light of our new media.

To be a reality-creator, is to have not only a purely personal, but also a social status in that production.

Reality may be a personal or collective product. Through the actions of one or many it can be set in motion.

Still, the validity of realities is commonly miscalculated by numbers of subscribers. Reality creation is therefore social power - as it always has been.

The number of adherents however, has no bearing on a reality's validity.

The creators of realities may have distinct desires separate from their subscribers.

Even so, the subscribers themselves have the power to become Reality-creators, or to change factors of the reality.

We rely on the market for realities to correct injustices here. The market must be truly open, unhindered, and dynamic.

In corporate dominated societies the past dominates the present.

In metaversal societies the present determines the meaning of the past.

In metaversal societies the past will in fact become both tangible and ultimately malleable.

The abolition of the past-dominated state will be decried by these prior beings as anarchy.

An abolition of culture!
An abolition of history!
An abolition of reason!

The metaversal citizen will reply that this state has already been upon us for some generations - the only difference being that the control over those perceptions now rests with the individual.

You are horrified that the past could become malleable - but in the existing society the past is just as fragile, and is now interpreted by just a select few editors.

You reproach us, that augmented realities could be as valid as the old perceived ones - but the only difference is that the new realities are becoming much richer.

In one word, you reproach us with intending to do away with your perceptions.

Precisely so - that is just what we intend.

From the moment that one's vision can become another's instantaneously, the enormous division between individuals - previously spanned by corporate interfaces - is ended.

From that moment you say, reason dissolves.

You must then confess that by reason you mean incorporated reason and reality - along with the owner of the ability to impose a reality within a monopoly.

This person must, indeed, be swept out of the way forever, and replaced by direct human connections.

It has been objected that upon the abolition of corporate realities all order will cease, and gang warlords bent on terror will overtake us.

The Reality-creators know that we are already dominated by corporate warlords - with singular names but wielding the power of thousands.

In this Reality-creators have a distinct task - to traverse a dangerous path through potential anarchy.

It will test one's preparedness to enter and create the new lands.

There will surely be criminals and casualties, heroes and victors, all the usual human stories amidst this revolution of perception.

We state that the market must remain open - accessible, and by this action these warlords will then be dealt with appropriately.

For those most attached to the sole, human Avatar this will be declared the destruction of all humans.

But these folk need not worry, as the entry into the realm of the virtual will be as gentle as one chooses to makes it.

It is the duty of the reality-creator to care deeply for the well being of the Avatar - human or as otherwise embodied.

Here in this Manifesto is where we in fact state the parameters which will make the transition palatable - and commit to this open market of realities as an essential prerequisite to proceed.

Those wishing social power will have to establish it anew.

Those wishing anonymity in their transactions should have that wish protected.

Reality-creators may appear to destroy – actually, they can only create and augment.

There is no place here for abuse of the power to create realities - and those that would try are most strictly opposed in our revolution.

You may say that it is the corporate media that protects us from repulsive and illegal content.

This is mistaken. It has not protected us at all from repulsive content and, in fact, has only been prohibited from selling such in as far as strong broadcast law applies.

For this, we again look to the market to determine the choices viewers make in their realities.

Guides, navigators, and groups will step forward in this new land to steer users.

Do you accuse us of displacing the center of the perceived universe away from a monolithic media? To this crime we plead guilty.

A top-down mass media that makes a mockery of human effort and dignity?

A nonstop barrage of scientifically engineered brainwashing?

Decades of lies and cover-ups financed by the select few owners of media dissemination?

Now, although they may own one or two passing venues - they can no longer own the content.

They have long degraded the very realities we seek to create as mere "content".

Sufficient only as the beast of burden for advertising messages.

No more.

The messages are dead. The "content" is what the market demands. The "content" what the market has always demanded. The corporate entities cannot deliver.

Their advertising can only work on a sleeping "target".

We are no longer targets and we are no longer sleeping.

The corporation does not even suspect that the point is to do away with their monolithic realities.

Composed as they are by Reality-creators themselves - now infected from within and terminal - these entities have no choice but to lose control of reality.

The corporation - the nation - the government - will be realized as the polite fictions adhered to only in desperation and deprivation – only when there was no alternative.

Reality-creators do not create dark matter "content", and we no longer choose realities in desperation.

Do not criticize Reality-creators for destroying national identity - that has already been largely accomplished by international corporations.

They have even used the human desire to improve living conditions entirely for their own growth, leaving self and family to degrade without regard to the cost. In this sense their aims are entirely apart from human aims.

No more.

Daily - internationally - individuals are connecting - talking - interacting and now building the Metaverse.

The supremacy of the international media makes it all the more venerable and obvious in its intent.

Make no mistake - every message you see in their media is a commercial. We cannot again fall into the established illusions, once liberated.

So great is the desire for person-to-person communication that thousands are even now devoting their lives and earning their living through our media.

Do not argue that corporate media has helped create this movement - any recognition of our movement itself by corporate media has happened only for their own promotional purposes.

Laughably, awkwardly, this pairing of identities has been solely to advance corporate interests.

No more.

The corporations cannot pair with their opposition. No matter how crafty the positioning.

The battle is already won by Reality-creators.

You may ask, is it not crucial that employment by corporate entities continue in order to maintain relative order?

The answer is a resounding yes - in fact, this is the very fabric of our revolution. Augmentation leaves older realities intact for those subscribers.

Do not mistake that this Metaverse Manifesto to advise disrupting order for those who wish it. Far from it.

We do not preach, convert, or monopolize. These are antithetical to our actions.

No one person or group can disturb the entire fabric of the economic system of international media - its very force will assimilate and then reposition that person.

This Manifesto speaks to the inhabitants of virtual worlds - and we realize the human to also live in a virtual world.

This is the person who will find meaning, and a place in new virtual worlds.

This revolution is the most radical in its application of technology to perception.

This revolution is the most gentle in its adaptability to individuals of all levels.

This revolution is the most empowering in its ability to augment the individual and her experience.

This revolution is the most obvious in the sense that all previous states of being are now becoming graphically visible.

Here the human person must accept that she already lives in a digitally created world.

Here the human person must accept that she is already an Avatar.

Here the Avatar must accept that we already exist in a virtual world of perceptions determined by a complex system of culture and experience, and media has almost exclusively created this.

In this Manifesto we state:

1. There is no objective reality whatsoever. There never has been.

2. Reality is the only commodity.

3. The Metaverse is not a simulation.

4. Digital information is now the only accepted format for "real" information. This is in fact already the state of being. What doesn't exist, virtually reproduced, does not exist.

5. Digital media defines all reality. Digital information describes all consensus realities. When science measures this reality, it relies solely on digital information. The digital Metaverse becomes the only reality platform.

6. Avatars are not a representation - they are appearances like any other. Persons exist as flesh. Persons exist as memories and experiences. As we record these experiences and share them through the digital network, persons exist as Avatars.

7. Our bodies are real to ourselves, as we perceive them. We will only be real to others as we appear as Avatars. In fact, it has always been this way - only now it is directly visible.

8. The most important revolution in perception brought about by computing technology has been the representation of one's "self" on a viewscreen.

9. Your attention of focus is the cursor. One's body then became the Avatar. Here we enter the virtual world - the digital landscape.

10. You have been augmented. Once augmented, you will not accept the previous state. This makes our revolution inevitable.

11. This representation of the self can be as simple as a cursor, or as complex as an Avatar or even an entire world. However it abides, it must remain infinitely malleable. This is the nature of the self-identity.

12. When we discuss the "Metaverse" or use other names for it, we are referring not only to a place that is created and perceived while augmented with computing technology - we are referring to perception itself as interpreted by the viewer.

13. The telescope augments the eye. The telephone augments the ear. The virtual world augments the projected being - it then revises and augments the being into a new form.

14. Virtualized three-dimensional spaces are revolutionary. This is not because they contain any technological advancement. It is due to the depiction of the space and the ability to see other viewers there. This has been the basis of "reality" since sense perception began.

15. Humans are hardwired to perceive in three dimensions - this is how we exist. Our senses have honed, over millions of years, the ability to perceive 3D landscapes,

forms and physiology. To us, this is "real". This makes our revolution inevitable.

16. This hardwired ability also accounts for the profound impact of seeing the Avatar in human (or other animated form). You see a being (animated) on a plane (land). The revolution lies in returning our basis of reality to this primordial interaction. In fact, this will eventually overthrow even the small screen itself.

17. We can no longer interact! We can no longer be real! The layers of definition in "real life" have been rendered an inhibited - recycled - stagnated - polluted experience.

We overthrow this with digital realities!

We destroy these appearances with networked and shared perceptions!

This new breed welcomes tomorrow.

We refuse the tyranny of top-down realities!

The network of individual Reality-creators is crucial to this Manifesto.

Free exchange remains the very fabric of this new world.

The new person is made, for new places.

Your Avatar is created.

We declare this a new land
     - with new inhabitants.

III. A COUP OF PERCEPTION

This Manifesto intends to overthrow key perceptions in order to make way for the freedom of Reality-creators.

The customizable Avatar itself is a more accurate representation of the being than the human form.

The human form is limited to existing within a certain set of cultures - within certain clothes and within certain times and locations.

All these limitations prohibit the mind from expanding, and have limited creativity.

We state that the Avatar is more "real" than the physical person.

This era now - sees the emergence of technologically defined realities and their inhabitants.

In the midst of this revolution - in the midst of this emergence - we realize the importance of the Avatar.

Previously defined as a cursor or spaceship - when this takes on the human form - and when the land takes on a familiar shape, the revolution in perception is achieved.

The perception passes through this portal.

The representation of space engages our perception - which has evolved over millions of years to see land, sky, water, people and animals and buildings.

From virtualized on the small screen, to immersive realities without any perceivable limitations - the revolution is now in motion.

Do not confuse this revolution as being aligned with "hackers", "open source" pressure groups, or "information wants to be free" pirates.

We stand for even more stern intellectual property respect and protections than the corporations ever did.

In previous times, theft from corporations was only perceived as acceptable due to the monopolistic abuses of that past.

This war has been largely won. The new Reality-creators are individuals. They must not be infringed.

We cannot accept violation of copyright protections and intellectual property. In fact, those that would do so undermine their own abilities and show themselves to be distinctly irrelevant in our new lands.

There is a central point to this revolution.

To infringe is to impede innovation - to recycle images is to poison to the culture.

These casualties of the recycled culture decades cannot bring their "creations" to these new lands. In fact, they are antithetical.

We now know, the "mass media" audience reads from a closed circle of about a dozen so called "journalists".

These corporate spokespersons are paid advertisers - they not impartial "journalists" as the dogma would preach.

We expose them.

All information is advertising.

All reality conflict is economic.

This Manifesto is read within a state of conflict - a state of motion - a state that opens the future.

This Manifesto reads within a state of insurrection for those that choose to join.

This insurrection is inward, where the reality forms itself. It is only outward for those who subscribe by choice.

We allow existing realities to remain unchanged.

War is in the air. But the air remains still as a spring day. Our revolution is the most radical in its openness.

We represent a revolution which opposes the cabal of self-congratulatory corporate interests.

Make no mistake - many Reality-creators will be paid by corporations to attempt to control reality once again.

This same state of affairs has existed as long as "the press" has existed. Nothing is new in this sense. This Manifesto exists as an impetus.

We believe in world communications.

We protect the personal interpretation of reality.

We welcome the era of spontaneous realities.

We reject corporate controlled realities.

In earlier times a body - a "corps" was needed to defend the physical tribe.

Even now, we will exist within groups, formed as they will be within new worlds.

We state that reality itself is user created - it always has been.

We bring to light the revolution now possible - as the receiver becomes augmented, aware, and awakens within the realm she has entered.

Artificial entities will also emerge as an important part of this landscape.

Already the "non-player character" is the person most frequently encountered in the various "worlds".

We recognize artificial intelligence as a key element to these new realities.

A myriad of realities have always been perceived and communicated between humans.

We also accept and welcome that parts of these realities themselves will be augmented by artificials.

The mode of communication is what has changed. Now, through computing technology, people are able to share their perceptions with large numbers of other people.

This is revolutionary.

Novels, paintings, plays, music, and other modes of human communication have always transmitted the perceptions of a given realities.

By relying on various levels of effort from the receiving person (by reading, viewing, etc.) these modes of communication served as conduits of perception from one person to another.

Now, we find available the ability to describe in immense detail, instantaneously, realities which would have only been personal perceptions.

The ancient struggle of sharing realities with others has been nearly won. We mean to destroy the remaining barriers to this.

This is revolutionary. This motion will not be stopped.

Time and space.
Limited being and place.
Disconnected and alone.
Immersed in illusion.

You have been fooled a thousand times without access to knowledge.

We declare this an unacceptable state!

We define a "reality": a set of perceptions and cues that combine to form an environment that is stable for a duration in time and is cognized by a being.

There is no limit to the number of perceivable realities. There never has been.

There is no "objective" reality. There never has been.

Knowledge of the existence of myriad realities is in itself a reality.

The number of subscribers to a particular reality does not validate it.

We struggle now, knowing many of the same struggles have been won before.

Only now the victory will be thorough - a complete coup of not only the perceptions but also the delivery and perceptive means themselves.

We have the common mission to liberate. We have the support and rallying cries of all but those who are afraid.

Our revolution has long been swelling, only now to become a recognizable force.

We have contempt for those who rule with deception
 - we will reveal them!

We have contempt for unlit and ignorant places
 - we will illuminate them!

We have contempt for sleep and for disconnectedness
 - we will destroy them!

We have disgust for limitations of all kinds
 - we will eliminate them!

With the new purpose we enter the new worlds.

We declare this a new way of being
 - with new purpose.

IV. REDUCTIONIST REACTIONS

In an unfortunate attempt to remain in control, there will be many reactions to this revolution, as indeed there already have been.

Why "virtual world"? Why "Metaverse"? "This is just the internet, really". Charges like these have been and will continue to be levied.

We are charged with "Alienation from Humanity," as if removing ourselves from the old order violated the rights of the old guard to sit motionless.

We are charged with "creating virtual goods," in "worlds that do not exist" by writers with their own virtual letters and words.

The critics fail by being concerned only with the immediate future. Comfortable in the present, they ensure their own irrelevance to the future.

Becoming a loud, dismissive, cynical critic is a proven pathway to fame and possibly fortune. There have never before been so many on this path - recycling their way to the past.

History has many times over exposed this species of parasite.

The reductionists fail to realize that ten years ago our type interaction and experience was relatively unthinkable.

The reductionists fail to recognize that a few experimental projects in the hands of a few programmers a few years ago, do not constitute a revolutionary change in perception on any measurable scale.

What happened then is history. A spark that ignited a few small fires. We stand now ablaze. This revolution is being experienced in new ways.

Our new lands reveal the telltale signs of an irreplaceable and crucial element.

This first sign is - that at first, it appears useless.

This second sign is - that at first, it appears redundant.

This third sign is - that at first, it is roundly opposed by the establishment.

Remember ancient history - every important technology was utterly useless - every world-changing view was called fiction.

Remember this going forward - every innovation will be refused - and its pioneers considered clowns.

Electronic communication was considered useful for scientists and teenagers, but certainly not for "business".

Now, it is the very fabric of every business. Now, we have converted into a complete digital reality.

The simulacra concept involved replication. The heroes and villains and artists of this period have had their day.

The Metaverse concept involves perception. The heroes and villains and artists of this time are now awakening.

Let us be blunt to all those who seek to control our perceptions.

The old fictions are no longer meaningful.

There is no more fiction.

The Metaverse is not a simulation.

The Metaverse is not a replication.

The Metaverse is not a representation of anything.

This revolution moves us from sharing expressions to sharing impressions.

Those who consider themselves "literate" will be especially repulsed by the new worlds, as they were with the earlier electronic revolutions.

Here again, we do not oppose them, or their way of life, except where they attempt to limit our movement.

The revolutionaries became the masters. Now the masters of the old concepts dismiss the Metaverse – this is because their skills are no longer revolutionary skills.

The old masters dismiss the Metaverse because it takes connectivity for granted.

These and other groups will be threatened by the coming Metaverse, and the inevitability of it will produce a strong dismissal and reactionist movements towards simplicity and the like.

We know these critics to be merely cheerleaders for a game that is already over and lost. Their own world is decaying, and this is frightening to them.

The loudest critics' words fall out of the virtual sky and melt like snow - they criticize worlds they have never entered.

Reality-creators have given up fear - have given up the old art forms - their detractors will stand corrected and left behind in history.

We know there will be those who discount our revolution - this is expected. Reductionists always have their own motives.

Mostly, they are subscribers to the default realities which we have thus far moved beyond.

Their motives are not separate from those who criticize us in other ways. In many cases, their minds may simply be too old. They are the "experts".

Criticism and detractors must be put in their own proper place - as part of the struggle of competing realities.

This is our primary advantage over previous revolutions. Our detractors struggle to limit themselves to no avail.

Our revolution does not affect them whatsoever. The critics rush to be a part of the Metaverse by hurling detractions at the unfamiliar.

We agree to let them decay in peace. Reality-creators will let them have their world intact. They simply have no relevant product for this new marketplace.

Our revolution abhors violence except as it applies to the uprooting of conditioned perceptions.

It is surprising though, that those, even who find themselves in the midst of naming these concepts themselves, would cling to the known rather than grasp the opening concepts.

Would be frightened rather than invigorated.

Would refuse the chance rather than take the chance.

To these we must say...

Never again, not in our worlds, is there a place for you.

This Manifesto will be denied by the forces that wish to control realities.

As you may have read, the revolution will not be televised.
The revolution will not be recycled.
The revolution will not be blogged.
The revolution will not be marketed.

The revolution will be live.

The revolution will be streamed and experienced.
The revolution is an experience.

The revolution will be shared amongst nodes, groups and individuals to each other.

Our time is real time.

As usual, the best adopters of new realities are those with little to lose. The greatest reactionaries are those will much to lose.

One will adapt and adopt. The other will become extinct. This is the nature.

Incumbent reality-lords will claim, "We created it!"
Incumbent voices will claim, "I thought of this!"
Incumbent leaders will say, "We originated this!"
Incumbent media will say "We have this for sale!"

You are a revolutionary - you must venture into what is emerging - you must dismiss the claims of old-reality "owners"

They wish to trap you and stop you as they did before - reality creators must not hold on to anything stationary.

They wish to trap all culture into a closed system that recycles tamed, static ideas.

Reactionaries will call the new realities "futile" and "fake"
      - not knowing their import.

Reductionists will call these statements "philosophy"
      - not experiencing their meaning.

Owners of all sorts of existing realties will stand fast
      - not knowing they are irrelevant.

These illusionists will continue to ply the age-old reality bases they dominate. For good reason, we have no use for them.

Ordinary persons will regard this revolution as common knowledge. The majority will simply pick up and use the new tools and realize the real boons to come.

We stand here on a new landscape - seeing it - knowing the wide-open spaces long before the cities and citizens and their stories arrive.

Inherent in this Metaverse Manifesto are the pure concepts of freedom of movement - of thought - of existence and of evolution itself.

Inherent in this Manifesto - the landscape is wild - unstable - unpredictable - and accessible to all.

Inherent in this experience - immersion - newness - intrigue.

We crave the violence of change

We declare this a new way of being.

We declare this an augmented reality - never again to be thought of as enduring!

V. YOU HAVE BEEN AUGMENTED

Joining into this revolution augments the person.

Refusing this revolution only postpones acceptance of it.

Our revolution will be the exclusive domain of the technologically connected for many years.

In the end, those that join and those that refuse may be considered separated - like two species.

To these two groups, objects will have different meanings.

To these two groups, history will have different stories.

There will be unintended consequences - just as the information revolution has had its own unintended and unpredictable consequences.

Various names are given to this phenomenon:
Some call it "The Metaverse".
Some call it "Virtual Reality".
Some call it "Virtual Worlds".
Some call it "The Matrix".
Some call it "Augmented Reality".

Other names, in other languages, will also be applied to it.

We are ready to end narrative fiction.

At the same time, we are ready to immerse ourselves in total, ultimate fictions. We welcome them as inevitable.

No longer should the perceiver be barred from the perception.

Through this revolution, we will both uncover and recover modes of perception that were considered lost or unprofitable.

The street name will not longer be the same for two persons. The country will no longer be the same for two "citizens" of it.

We announce that this is good for human beings. We announce that we must accept these new modes.

At such time that this movement takes hold, the thousands of realities will become visible.

At such time the creators of realities will have become interlinked.

At such time perception will not be limited by time or distance.

Even this Metaverse - even this set of universes - will at that time, be superseded by even more profound abilities.

This class has long run underground - derided by both the corporate reality mongers and even the technologists themselves.

A forerunner of this class feared losing the old realities. Despite their fear, they lost them. Now, this new breed realizes it has nothing to lose.

Whether intended or not the technology fell into the hands of these revolutionaries - there was no other option.

The cogs in the wheels of the corporate juggernauts were themselves composed of these revolutionary creators.

Even now some creators themselves model themselves as the corporations, and remain engaged in monopolistic wars.

Yet few have the resources to pitch such a battle - largely they are won not even in the minds of the subscribers but in court battles.

The system has no future - and such fraudulent attempts to control reality will be exposed.

Subsistence tribal economy gave way to feudal economy and the power shifted to the landlords.

Feudal agricultural economy gave way industrial economy and the power shifted to the capitalists.

Industrial economy gave way to the information economy and the power shifted to the programmers.

Information economy give way to the attention economy and the power shifted to celebrity information recyclers.

Attention economy gives way to the perception economy and the power is shifting to the Reality-creators.

Still more economies will follow! This is the organic nature of our revolution.

So powerful is this new era, that it enables the recreation of even extinct economies. So powerful are these new abilities that they can encompass and augment all prior reality structures.

These are things to come.

The old guard aggregators will post these insights up for view as if they are their own ideas.

The old corporate media will post these insights as their own product.

They will claim that this is part of their own "media" revolution - in fact; they already have begun this insolent plagiarism.

We know that nothing could be further from the truth.

They are part and particle of what must be destroyed.

Recognize them by their attempts to appropriate our insights and pose as Reality-creators.

We refuse their decaying regurgitated mass perceptions.

Our realities may or may not be Utopian.
Our realities may or may not be walled gardens.
Our realities may or may not be widely interlinked.

The crucial element is that Reality-creators are not engaged in monopolistic struggle.

Either way, the old guard will oppose us.

Technologists will curse the walled gardens - due to their own economic struggle towards relevance.

Open sourcers will demand free code - recalling the tyranny of the lowest common denominator.

Wishing to retain control they will hack and attempt to usurp any reality which is adverse or in opposition to their own.

What they do not know is that their energy is spent opposing an unstoppable cascade.

We do not fight them except by continuing to create.

Our actions themselves render the old realities inert. Our actions themselves defeat without battle. This is the core of our Manifesto.

These powers attempt annexation in the same way in which a foreign language is appropriated, namely, by translation.

The wares, however, do not fit the market.

The antique goods arrived, dragging along only the old buyers.

We therefore apply a revolutionary economy, which will lead to new societies.

The old social laws will seem to break down, as new viewers are augmented into new histories.

The histories themselves will of course seek to establish and maintain realities - what else could they do?

Long ago the historians themselves were corrupted, and the "information" they spewed became advertising.

But now as never before, the path of choice will be open - a link away - and the task will fall to Reality-creators to stabilize their worlds.

Yet, true Reality-creators recognize that even this is not their ultimate duty.

At every turn they must avoid the solidification and stagnation that plagued earlier epochs!

The undeveloped state of the field of realities will be unorganized, chaotic, and meaningless at first.

But even undeveloped, the view of possibilities is unlimited, and can only be called fantastic.

The first instinctive yearnings of that class will be for a general reconstruction of realities and reorganization of the meaning of the terms themselves.

At this point we will recognize the fruits of our early efforts.

Reality-creators fight for the attainment of these immediate aims:

We support the existing virtual worlds as pioneering platforms - valid in their own right - and as decisive victories against corporate realities.

We support the alternative reality builders and game realities and welcome them to apply their skills in ever more effective ways.

We support the augmented reality pioneers - early insurgents waging war with few funds and immense opposition.

We support above all the viewer - the participant - we pledge ourselves that their interest is ours, or that their exit not be obstructed.

In short, the Reality-creators everywhere support every revolutionary movement against the existing corporate described order of perceptions.

In all these movements we bring to the front, as the leading question in each, the objective of enabling the steering of reality - no matter what its degree of its development at the time.

Reality-creators disdain to conceal their views and aims.

They openly declare that their ends can be attained only by the forcible overthrow of all existing corporate owned realities within the viewer.

Let the ruling media owners tremble at a "virtual" revolution.

The viewers have nothing to lose but their limitations.

They have endless worlds to win.

REALITY CREATORS OF ALL PLATFORMS - CREATE!

Interview with Orange Montagne:

By Indigo Paperclip

Indigo Paperclip: Orange, what is the Metaverse Manifesto?

Orange Montagne: The Metaverse Manifesto is a statement of both reality and of intent. This generation has been devoid of statements and devoid of vision - this generation has been devoid of anything but momentary recycled cultural images.

It was important to state this now - time is of the essence. We need to create and interconnect realities, first on the small screen, then, through augmentation. These are the early days. I want to get the discussion and innovation going. This is the most exciting time to be alive, and the coming years will be even more wild. Today, MMOG's. Perception itself is next.

Indigo Paperclip: It sounds like you are part of a big group with all the "we shall" stuff. Are you really leading some kind of revolution?

Orange Montagne: Here I'm defining the moment and stating the aims and shared interest of Reality-creators. It is a moment in time, and a very important moment. The new worlds are wide open and with these motivations we can take this time and make it a revolutionary time. Again, this is also inevitable. But it is crucial to separate this from the old "entertainments" that rotted and expired so long ago.

Indigo Paperclip: Ok, Orange, as an Avatar, what am I supposed to do after reading this?

Orange Montagne: No worries Indigo, this is an amazing time! I'll make the prediction that, in just a few years, the five most important people in your life that you interact with the most will be people you never met in person. It may already be like that for thousands of people!

In seven years an artificially intelligent friend will be a very important part of your day and of your world. I don't even address that in the Manifesto because it's a separate issue. Get ready to be part of history.

Indigo Paperclip: You seem to be saying that an era of "corporate controlled realities is ending". But don't those same powerful entities control the whole internet anyway?

Orange Montagne: Yes of course much of the infrastructure is owned and manufactured by corporations. I'm not anti-corporation in the traditional sense you may be used to. I'm a supporter of creating new realities and this technology is allowing that to happen. We are stating that this process is better now, and time to leave the old world behind. We can of course light our revolutionary meetings with the same electricity used for toasters. As I state, this revolution leaves the old realities in place. Virtual worlds operate like this.

Indigo Paperclip: I'm just a normal girl, Orange. Is there anything I need to do differently?

Orange Montagne: Try to back things like "net neutrality", which is key to the entire world communication and economic system, and something Avatars should push for. Of course the old guard will try again and again to shut this down and impose their controls.

We are living what would be considered a science fiction. Science has created and enabled these new "fictions". Yet, they are not fictions at all, they are real experiences. This is occurring simultaneously and almost silently alongside the "meatspace".

The old culture is over, seriously over. Generations coming up will regard what we used to call "history" as a derivative work based on an anime or other "fictional" world. In their minds, there is already no difference. And why should there be?

I can see on the horizon, a vast conflict. An epic war of realities culminating in a violent overthrow of the tyranny of conditioned perceptions of all kinds.

The Metaverse Manifesto has some very deep points to it —
yet it is presented in an entertaining way - I simply can't get
bogged down in academic speak during this exciting time. I
don't think readers would want to either.

Indigo Paperclip: Thanks Orange, best wishes as this all
unfolds.

The Metaverse Manifesto - a statement of how digital realities have become the only realities.

The book is an indispensable guide to new media and the emerging phenomenon of the "Metaverse".

With the Metaverse Manifesto, Avatar Orange Montagne states the mission of the new creative breed he calls Reality-creators.

They reject and then supersede established media and recycled culture. The core of their revolutionary actions is focused on creating immersive places.

Destroying "fictions", they create spaces that include the viewers themselves, viewers that had previously been locked out of the media they perceived.

Written by Orange Montagne, a pioneer explorer in the concepts of the "digital being".

With this Manifesto, the implications of user-generated content are shown to extend much further than they do today, up to the point of describing the very realities we now inhabit.

Volatile - impulsive – wild - written during a time of revolution and struggle to define the spaces called "virtual worlds."

Definition:

http://en.wikipedia.org/wiki/Metaverse

"The Metaverse contains the Multiverses and all universes past and present."

Publisher:

http://www.studiosfo.com

Our other publications:

Acedia's Avatar Fashion Series

Acedia's Avatar Fashion Calendars

Transmudream Series

Printed in the United States
114668LV00008B/313/A